Mishawak

EXAM
BUSTING

Sam Morgan

summersdale

EXAM-BUSTING TIPS

First published in 2005
Reprinted 2006
This edition copyright © Summersdale Publishers Ltd, 2014

Summersdale Publishers Ltd
46 West Street
Chichester
West Sussex
PO19 1RP
UK

www.summersdale.com

Printed and bound in the Czech Republic

ISBN: 978-1-84953-539-7

Substantial discounts on bulk quantities of Summersdale books are available to corporations, professional associations and other organisations. For details contact Nicky Douglas by telephone: +44 (0) 1243 756902, fax: +44 (0) 1243 786300 or email: nicky@summersdale.com.

CONTENTS

INTRODUCTION

For many people, sitting exams represents all that is daunting in the world of academia. The months, weeks, days or minutes of revision that you have put in, probably with a degree of reluctance, all build up to the stress that is the day of the exam.

But help is at hand. If you dread the impatient shuffling outside the exam hall while you wait to be called in, relax. If you fear being surrounded by people claiming to be either 'terrified', 'on the verge of a nervous breakdown' or, conversely but just as bad, 'absolutely ready for any topic that should arise', breathe easy. And if you have ever been known to go into an exam with only one pen, then don't panic, my under-equipped friend — all is by no means lost.

You too can be part of that group of people who walk into the exam room calm and confident and ready to achieve their best.

GETTING STARTED

First things first – you need to address what your goals are, and work out a plan for achieving them.

THE POWER WITHIN

In order to succeed in passing exams and obtain the best possible result, you must make a conscious decision to maximise your potential and create within yourself resources of willpower and self-motivation. You've taken the first step by picking up this book. Once you have made this decision, you will need to apply consistent effort throughout the entire revision process, and this book will show you how.

WHAT'S YOUR OBJECTIVE?

Most people will answer this question with something like 'I want to pass', 'I want to get an A' or 'I will be happy just to get through it'. It is far more helpful to have smaller, more immediate goals, such as: 'I will feel confident in my knowledge of Topic X by next Friday', or even smaller-scale goals, such as: 'For the next twenty minutes I will make notes on Topic X and then I will spend an hour writing up an essay.' Of course, you want to stay focused on your overall goal – to pass your exam – but breaking it down into small steps will help you to get there more effectively.

IT'S ALL ABOUT DISCIPLINE

Good self-discipline is what is going to get you the highest grades. You need to balance your social, family and work commitments so that you remain calm and focused and – most importantly – sane. Bestselling author Anthony Trollope wrote forty novels whilst working full-time as the general manager of a post office, by working during office breaks, on trains or at breakfast. With a little effort, you too can be equally productive.

PLANNING YOUR REVISION

Remember the 6 Ps: proper prior planning prevents poor performance.

PLAN AHEAD

The run-up to exam time can be daunting, particularly if you're trying to tackle more than one subject at a time. The first thing you need to do is plan. Make or buy yourself a calendar that shows the weeks and (hopefully) months between now and the exam(s). Find out the dates, times and locations of each of your exams and fill them in on the appropriate place on your calendar. If the exam is focused on one particular topic, write this down too.

BLOCK IN THE BASIC STRUCTURE OF YOUR TIMETABLE

This is the easy part: divide each day of the week on your timetable into hourly slots, and fill in all of your current commitments — whether it's school, lectures, work, babysitting, clubs or sports. After you have allowed for meals and relaxation, you'll be able to see how much spare time you have each day to dedicate to revising.

LIFESTYLE REVIEW

Only you will know when you can work at your optimal level. You must be honest with yourself when deciding this and possibly make some important lifestyle changes. If you work best in the morning but like to sleep in late, then for the duration of the exam period you should consider going to bed earlier so you can get up earlier and maximise the efficiency of your work.

PEAK PRACTICE TIME

Ask yourself these questions before you fill in the rest of your timetable:

- Do you prefer to study early in the morning, during the day or late at night?

- During which part of the day have you carried out your strongest work?

- How can you motivate yourself to work at this time every day?

LENGTH OF STUDY PERIODS

The ideal length of each study period can differ from person to person but to find out what works best for you, try varying the amount of time you spend revising at the start of your revision programme. Test yourself to see how well you have absorbed what you have been studying and use the results to decide on a time frame which suits you. A reasonable guideline is to spend 45 minutes to one hour at a time revising.

PRIORITISE YOUR SUBJECTS

If you know that you'll need more time to get to grips with your biology notes than your history ones, biology will be higher on your list of priorities. This doesn't mean you should avoid those lower down on the list, but it will help you work out how much revision time to allocate to each subject.

PRIORITISE YOUR MODULES

You should also break each exam down into the separate modules that are likely to be covered. The modules you feel less comfortable with should be allocated more revision time than the ones you already know fairly well, and you should revise the toughest bits first. Look at this as getting the hardest things out of the way first – once you've jumped that hurdle it will only get easier!

MIX IT UP

Make sure when you fill in your various subjects that you don't allocate one three-hour slot to the same subject. If you have three hours to fill, most people will find it far more useful to spend 45 minutes each on three different topics, with a 15-minute break in-between to stretch your legs, get a drink and allow the information to sink in.

AN EVEN BALANCE

Make sure you balance the subjects you enjoy the most against the ones you find hardest, or take the least pleasure in. You're far more likely to sit down and revise one of your toughest subjects well if you know that it's only for an hour, and then you'll be turning to something you feel more confident in.

TOP TIP

TIMING IS KEY

Put the tasks that you think will take
the most energy and effort at your
peak times for concentrating – so
if you work best first thing in the
morning, it would be logical to start
the day with the toughest task when
you'll be able to tackle it at
your optimum.

GIVE YOURSELF REGULAR BREAKS

Once you have decided on an optimal time frame for each revision session, it is important to remember to book in regular breaks. This is especially true at weekends, when you're likely to have more time and may get overly ambitious. While you may feel you need to spend every spare second revising, it will benefit you far more in the long run if you allow time for recreational activities. This will allow your brain to recompose itself between chunks of revision and help you absorb what you've been studying.

COLOUR CODING

Some people find it useful to colour code their revision timetable. It helps you see at a glance which topics you've got coming up, and can help when you're planning to make sure you haven't bunched the same subject together on any one day. It can be good to take pride in your timetable, but it's not a work of art – don't waste time that could be spent revising making your timetable a masterpiece!

ASK FOR ADVICE

Your teacher or tutor should be able to give you advice on organising your revision. From offering you guidance on which topics they feel you need to focus on the most, to giving you tips from their years of experience in preparing other students for exams, it's often worth asking for their help.

SET SMART GOALS

The goals you set for yourself should be SMART: Specific, Measurable, Attainable, Relevant and Time-bound.

- Specific: make sure you have broken down your topic into individual chunks, and have a definite outcome in mind, e.g. 'I want to fully understand how to find a square root.'

- Measurable: find ways to test whether you have achieved your goal, e.g. by using practice papers.

- Attainable: you should always strive for your best, but your goal should be within your reach.

- Relevant: you should be focusing on things you know may come up in the exam.

- Time-bound: set yourself a time limit – 'I want to have achieved this by the end of Monday.'

APPS

There are some useful apps which can help you plan your revision, as well as helping you to learn the topics themselves. Only use these if you feel they will be of real benefit – for some people they may end up being more of a distraction than a help.

TRIAL AND ERROR

Once you've planned your revision, you may sit down to the first session and realise that something's not quite right – maybe you should be revising in the evening, rather than the morning, or you should be allocating shorter study periods. All that is fine; you can simply adjust your timetable to make it work. Everyone learns differently, and working out what's best for you is a learning curve.

OVERCOMING REVISION HURDLES

It can be easy to find excuses to avoid revising, or ways to procrastinate once you've officially started a revision session. Recognition is the first step in dealing with this problem – if you can identify the root of your problem, you can tackle it head-on.

IDENTIFY YOUR ANXIETIES

Examine the following statements, be honest with yourself about which apply to you and then tick them accordingly. If necessary, add any others that you think are important in the spaces provided. Revisit these pages regularly to assess your revision progress.

- [ ] I sleep badly during a revision period
- [ ] I find it difficult to begin revising
- [ ] I think I am going to fail
- [ ] I can't stick to my timetable
- [ ] I can't concentrate on my revision
- [ ] I forget what I have just learnt
- [ ] I think everyone else is more confident
- [ ] I don't work hard enough
- [ ] I don't start revising early enough
- [ ] I get bored
- [ ] I sometimes feel I should give up completely

....

....

....

I SLEEP BADLY DURING A REVISION PERIOD

- Get up earlier in the morning, and avoid taking naps during the day, so that you're ready for a full night's sleep by evening.

- Exercise is a great way of ensuring you feel tired at the end of the day. Do it early in the evening so that your body has time to cool down before you try to sleep, and you'll enjoy not only the benefits of a good night's sleep, but also the proven stress relief it provides.

- Avoid caffeine, tobacco and alcohol, as they contain stimulants that will only make it that much harder to drift off. If you find it hard to go without a hot drink before bed, try warm milk or herbal or decaf tea.

- Make your bedroom a haven for sleep: make sure it's ventilated and cool, with as little noise and light as possible. Remove electronic devices or items that create artificial light from your bedroom if possible, so that the room is dark and cosy and you don't associate it with anything but sleep. Use an eye mask and earplugs if necessary.

- Taking a warm bath, having a massage, or even just rubbing your stomach and toes can relax you and make you feel sleepy.

- Visualise a peaceful scene, breathe deeply and practise progressive relaxation – tense and then release the muscles in your body working from your feet up to your neck and shoulders, then down your arms to the palms of your hands. You'll feel relaxed and serene.

I FIND IT DIFFICULT TO BEGIN REVISING

The best way to conquer this problem is to schedule your revision and stick to it. You will have decided on a time when you will start revising – when you'll be sure to have no distractions – and how long the study session will last in your timetable. Make sure you are sitting down with your books out from the scheduled time, and reward yourself when you get to the end of the session (a nice cup of tea and a biscuit, perhaps). Successful revision depends on self-motivation – nobody can do it for you. Once you have managed that much, the whole process will become much easier than you think.

I THINK I AM GOING TO FAIL

Once you have consciously made the decision to pass your exams and have begun some serious revision, you will find that you are able to replace this thought with 'I know I am going to pass.' Reading this book is a step in the right direction! Every hour of revision you do increases your changes of exam success. Studies have shown that those who visualise themselves succeeding at their particular obstacle are likely to do far better than those who visualise failure, so try to stay positive!

I CAN'T STICK TO MY TIMETABLE

Most people find revision difficult, but if you want to achieve good grades then it must be done. View your timetable as a full-time work schedule rather than an optional outline for your day. The consequences for not following the timetable can be just as great as if you were to get into trouble at work. Reward yourself on completion of chunks of revision.

I CAN'T CONCENTRATE ON MY REVISION

Many people have difficulty maintaining their attention span over an extended period of time. During revision periods, the problem can be avoided by taking regular breaks, eating and drinking well to keep your energy levels high, breaking your revision up into chunks, working in good lighting conditions (preferably daylight if possible) and making sure your work environment is at a comfortable temperature.

I FORGET WHAT I HAVE JUST LEARNT

If you find yourself staring blankly at notes you have just written, unable to comprehend their meaning, then take a break or change topics. Your revision plan should provide variation amongst the topics you need to revise; not only from day to day, but preferably hour to hour. There is a reason that schools vary their timetables – people cannot maintain their learning focus on one subject for an extended period of time. By regularly changing revision topic and taking breaks, this problem should be avoided.

I THINK EVERYONE ELSE IS MORE CONFIDENT

The solution is simple: take no notice. The people who come across with the most confidence and bravado are normally the people who are actually the most nervous and have done the least amount of study. People behave differently under stressful conditions and exam time is no exception. There's no way of knowing how someone else is really feeling, so concentrate on your own study and make sure that your confidence comes from being satisfied with the amount of effort you have put in.

I DON'T WORK HARD ENOUGH

You may be feeling this way for one of two reasons:

1. You have worked yourself up into a state of panic and have in fact done more work than you think.

2. You genuinely haven't done enough work and need to step it up a little.

In some cases, the first instance may be more problematic than the second. If you feel yourself becoming neurotic about your revision, then slow down and take a break because the chances are that the amount of information you are absorbing is decreasing rapidly. Successful revision is not about the number of hours you spend revising but about your approach and commitment to a programme of well-planned, regular study.

If you fall into the second category then you really need to work harder. Following the tips in this book should help!

I DIDN'T START REVISING EARLY ENOUGH

If you cram your revision into just a few days before each exam you will almost certainly not achieve a high grade. It is impossible to absorb information at that rate and you will be lucky to retain even ten per cent of what you revise. Give yourself a reasonable amount of time to cover all of the topics that may come up in your exams. Regularly return to and retest yourself on previous topics and you will find that you absorb your revision much more efficiently.

I GET BORED

If you view revision as a tedious task that's eating into your free time and harming your social life, start adjusting the way you think. Focus instead on what passing this exam will achieve – a fulfilling career, perhaps, or self-satisfaction. Take interest in your subject, and think of your revision sessions as a fascinating insight into a new area of knowledge. If you're actively engaged with the topic and can get excited about all the new things you're learning, you should be able to stop viewing revision as such a chore.

I SOMETIMES FEEL I SHOULD GIVE UP COMPLETELY

Never! If you are feeling like this then talk to your friends, teachers or parents, or call any of the counselling advice lines offered by most colleges and universities. There are people who are trained to help if you are in this state of mind. Don't be embarrassed about asking for assistance or feeling a little low, because you certainly won't be the first person to have experienced this.

REVISION RESOURCES

There are lots of places you can turn for help. Here is just a selection of the useful resources you should use in your revision.

PAST PAPERS

Look at past exam papers as it is usually fairly easy to identify a pattern in topics that have arisen in the past and therefore may arise again. Discuss your findings with the relevant tutor – they may not be able to help you specifically, but will certainly give you an idea of whether you are moving in the right direction. Past papers are particularly useful for analysing the style and construction of exam questions, but beware of any syllabus changes that may have been introduced this year – you could ask your tutor for advice.

COURSE NOTES

Look back over course notes and divide it up into topics or subject headings. Doing this will enable you to spread your revision topics out over a well-planned timetable. If you have taken notes during the course then make sure you have a full set. It can be a useful exercise to check your set of notes with a friend on the same course.

TOP TIP

TUTORS

Speaking to a tutor about topics you don't understand is invaluable. Discuss any problems you are having with them, and they should be able to guide you in the right direction. Remember, your tutor wants you to perform well, so you should value their time and advice.

THE INTERNET

There is a wealth of information online, from specific revision websites such as the BBC's 'Bitesize' resource and the exam companies' own sites, to more general resources such as online encyclopedias – Wikipedia is the most popular, but may not always be the most reliable. Check websites such as Britannica.co.uk and Encyclopedia.com to verify any information you find online.

WHERE SHOULD I REVISE?

The most important thing to consider when choosing where to revise is your comfort, and a suitable lack of distractions. You'll want to be able to work undisturbed and in peace for a fairly long stretch of time, with ample light (natural if possible), so it's important that you find somewhere you can relax. There's a benefit to varying the location of your revision sessions, so that you can build up a variety of memory cues — different sights, sounds and smells that may jog your memory when it comes from the actual exam.

Some places you could try include at home, at a library or outside.

NO PLACE LIKE HOME

For most people, home is where the majority of revision takes place. We are naturally at ease in comfortable and familiar surroundings where we can control the temperature and volume levels, have easy access to food and drink, and can work undisturbed. If you think it would be helpful, give the people you live with a copy of your revision timetable and ask them to respect your need for peace during the times you have allocated for study at home.

THE LIBRARY

The library can be an excellent place to revise. Here, it is possible to access a wealth of information when you are unsure about certain aspects of your revision. However, libraries can be daunting places and are often full of distractions such as friends and acquaintances if it is the institution's own library, and there's the danger of being sucked into all those books! The majority of your revision should be uninterrupted and conducted privately (although group revision can be useful – more on that later).

THE GREAT OUTDOORS

Sometimes revising outside can be a refreshing change. Revising in parks, for instance, can be very peaceful. However, be warned – on a windy day your notes may be blown away and you could find yourself spending more time chasing after them than actually revising!

If you do choose this option it is a good idea to move around during your revision, as it will help freshen up your attention levels. When you have a break, try taking a stroll.

REVISION TECHNIQUES

Now you've worked out where and when you're going to study, it's time to get down to some actual revision! These tips should help you on your way to effective and efficient revision.

TOP TIP

BE ACTIVE

The most important point to remember when revising is that any revision you do must be active. Simply reading and rereading your notes is a passive approach and you will retain far less information than if you use active revision techniques. Furthermore, active revision is far more likely to be enjoyable, and this is important if you want to maximise the amount of information you take in. The following tips are all examples of revising actively.

WAYS OF REVISING

Everybody works slightly differently; make time to find out what works for you. Your revision may be most efficient when you simply read the textbook or your notes and then write down what you've learned. However, some people work better with images rather than words (in this case, making spider diagrams or drawing out concepts and ideas could be useful); some people find it helpful to teach what they have learnt to others, as it means you have to find new ways to elaborate on the information you're learning.

DIAGRAMS AND TABLES

Draw diagrams and pictures and make tables of your information. They will be much easier to bring to mind and make it easier to distinguish patterns and connections than pages of similar-looking notation. Even if you are studying an arts subject and usually express your thoughts in words, you would be surprised how many subjects can be illustrated visually, and these images will stick in your mind ready for access on the day of the exam.

MIND MAPPING

Also known as spider diagrams or brainstorms, these are excellent visual representations of the way that the brain deals with information. Try writing down a subject heading in the middle of the page and then add branches to help you see the connections between different aspects of your subject. It can be good to do this at the start of your revision process, so you can revise your way around the mind-mapped topics logically, going from one connection to the next.

MNEMONICS

Mnemonics are a good way of remembering important phrases or quotes by using abbreviations, words or rhyming phrases. A common example is the method of teaching the fates of Henry VIII's six wives through this rhyme:

Divorced, beheaded, died
Divorced, beheaded, survived

When making up your own, the more unique the better – you'll be more likely to remember it if you have some fun making it up!

SING IT!

If there's a particularly important quotation, formula or concept you are struggling to remember, try singing it to the tune of a catchy song. It sounds silly, but if you can find a way of making the words fit to a tune, it's far easier to remember the name of a song than an entire paragraph of text – you can then sing through the song until it all comes back to you.

REVISING WITH OTHERS

Group revision sessions are helpful opportunities to discuss any doubts you have about anything you are revising. Often a quick discussion will clear up any problems with a topic that you might have and can also be valuable practice in how to approach structuring an essay on that topic. Do double check any information you friends offer, though – they may not completely grasp the concept either! However, this type of revision session should not feature too heavily in your revision programme as distractions can prove more difficult to resist when in a group.

TACKLE AN EASY
JOB FIRST

If you start your revision session with a task you know you can accomplish, it will give you a boost of motivation and get you in the right frame of mind for learning. Unfortunately, this doesn't work if you focus only on the easy things for the rest of the session, as you'll end up with a pile of your least favourite topics left to tackle – so make sure you follow the easy starter with a more intensive subject.

THIRSTY WORK

Keep yourself well hydrated in order to help maintain your attention and focus. More than half of your body is made up of water, and your body needs a good amount of water to enable it to transport nutrients and oxygen around the body, flush out waste products and help with digestion. An average adult needs between 1½ and 2 litres of water per day. If you're not keeping hydrated, you'll feel groggy and unable to concentrate, and may suffer from headaches which will prevent you from revising – so drink up!

CARRY A NOTEBOOK AND MAKE USE OF YOUR SMARTPHONE

This will help you to make the most of those small pockets of 'free' time, such as standing in post office queues or waiting for a bus. If, for example, you were able to learn three mathematical equations per day by doing this, then over a month you would have learnt ninety new equations. There are note-taking apps on most smartphones these days, so there's never an excuse to be unable to revise!

LEAD US NOT INTO TEMPTATION

There will be occasions when you become tempted by activities more appealing than a few hours at the books. These can vary from trips with friends and shopping excursions to more inane distractions such as suddenly getting the urge to scrub your bathroom clean or organise your CDs by alphabet and genre. If this is a weakness of yours, the best thing is not to go 'cold turkey'. Instead schedule yourself set times for leisure and social activities and use that time as a reward for all the hard work you've done.

STEP AWAY FROM THE COMPUTER

It's all too easy to get sucked in to the dreaded spiral – you 'quickly' check one of your social media accounts and then, many hours and websites later, you finally re-emerge into the real world. The best way to prevent this is to avoid the Internet for all but revision-based activities altogether. Sign out of Facebook and Twitter (you could ask someone you trust to change the passwords temporarily while you're revising), leave your phone in another room so you're not tempted to check it constantly, and start working.

LISTENING TO MUSIC

As long as it doesn't disrupt your concentration, it's OK to listen to music while you revise. It's best to listen to music without words as they can be quite a distraction when trying to absorb particularly taxing subjects.

TOP TIP

TICK OFF PROGRESS

Make sure that as you work through the revision you have set out for yourself, you tick off each topic or completed revision period. It will give you a confidence boost to see how far you've come.

IF YOU SLIP UP

If, for some reason, you miss a study period or just find that you really can't get on and concentrate, don't beat yourself up. These things happen, and there's always a way around them. Instead of going shopping with your friends at the weekend, swap it for a cup of coffee and a chat so you can spend the extra hour or two catching up on revision. If you can't get out of other commitments, you could always wake up an hour earlier than usual to catch up, but try not to make this a habit.

TEST YOURSELF

At the end of each week's revision, you should schedule in a mock test for each of the topics you've been revising. These can be actual practice papers from the exam providers, past papers you may have been given in class, or just questions you think are likely to come up. You don't have to do a whole exam every week, but by submitting yourself to exam conditions (time yourself, don't talk to anyone and turn off your phone) and writing, you'll not only be reinforcing what you've learnt, but also getting in good practice for the real thing.

REWARDS

Reward yourself on completion of a successful day's or week's revision. It can boost morale and provide welcome relief from studying. Eating a nice meal, watching your favourite film or having a drink with friends can be a much-appreciated reward.

TIME TO RELAX

It's important that you don't let your revision take over your life. Take time to relax, and you'll go into your exam prepared and healthy!

VEG OUT

There is no point revising all day every day as your brain will overload and your revision will become inefficient. Give yourself time to lie on the sofa and switch off. Watch your favourite soaps or turn on your games console and hammer those buttons.

GO OUT ON THE TOWN

Remember you are not alone in having to revise. Reward yourself and your friends with some fun and relaxation at the end of a sustained period of revision (this period should be measured in days – not hours!).

TALK, TALK, TALK

If you have concerns, or are feeling anxious about any aspect of your revision or exam taking, it is a good idea to talk about it. Discussing your problems with friends, family and teachers is a good way to relieve some of that tension. Meet up with friends to discuss any issues that have arisen, or anxieties in your life. A problem shared is a problem halved, and an exam period is no time to be sitting on problems.

TOP TIP

READ – FOR FUN!

It may be the last thing you want to do, but don't forget how rewarding it can be to read a book solely for pleasure. Lose yourself in the fantastical pages of a great novel or in the faraway lands of an exciting travel memoir – but do try to put it down before your next study session begins!

CATCH A FILM

There is nothing like a good movie to take your mind off the books. Venture out to the cinema and distance yourself from your revision space. This will enable you to have a really clean break from studying and return with a much clearer mind.

TIDY UP

Working in messy surroundings often causes a feeling of claustrophobia or anxiety. Keep your revision area clear and tidy, and give your mind a break from revision at the same time.

LOOK AFTER YOUR BODY

Healthy body, healthy mind. If you look after your physical well-being then your mind will be sharper and more active and you will absorb your revision much more efficiently.

BANISH THOSE NERVES

Everybody gets a little nervous at the prospect of important exams – it's only natural. Luckily there are some tricks and techniques you can use to make sure they don't hold you back.

RELISH THE NERVES

Being a little nervous before an exam puts your body in a slightly hyper state, fuelled by adrenalin that heightens your concentration and performance. Lots of performers use the power of the 'fight or flight' mechanism to achieve great heights in their work, so don't be scared of the feeling – harness it and use it to your advantage.

KEEP AN EYE ON STRESS

Don't ignore worries about your exam. Stress can build up as multiple factors combine until you can't cope any more, so try to deal with every problem as it occurs so that the stress is always manageable. This also applies to stresses of everyday life – keep them under control and you'll find you can cope with your exams too.

EAT THE RIGHT THINGS

A balanced diet of natural and healthy foods will help your body to cope with stress more easily. Too much sugar or caffeine will exacerbate any feelings of stress you may have.

EAT CHOCOLATE

Despite chocolate's high sugar content there are a multitude of benefits to eating a few squares of dark chocolate every day. Studies suggest that dark chocolate can relieve stress and anxiety, improve mood and cognitive function and even create a sense of peace and relaxation.

TOP TIP

BREATHE

If the looming exam causes anxiety, try breathing techniques. It's simple, but surprisingly effective: breathe in deep, hold for a few seconds, breathe out. Repeat several times, and focus on nothing but your breathing. It helps to empty your mind of worries and calms your heart rate.

BELIEVE IN YOURSELF

You can do it. You've worked hard for this. You have probably absorbed more information than you think. Think of a couple of particularly good revision sessions you've had recently, and take pleasure in the thought of showing off your knowledge to the examiner who marks your exam.

MEDITATE

Find five minutes each day in the week before the test to sit in a quiet place, close your eyes, and let your mind take you to place of calm and serenity; perhaps a beach where the waves are lapping at your toes and the sun is warming your body. This will help to prevent a build-up of pre-test nerves.

THE DAY OF THE EXAM

The day has arrived! The lead-up to an exam can be a very nerve-wracking time, but the following pages will help you stay calm as you prepare for the big day itself.

THE NIGHT BEFORE

Pack your bag. Check and recheck that you have all the equipment necessary to sit your exam. Check that your pens work and take spares and a pencil. If you are using a calculator, there is no harm in replacing the batteries as part of your preparation. Also remember to pack any drinks or sweets that you wish to take – a bottle of water is essential.

ALARM BELLS

Make sure that you have a back-up alarm. It is probably unlikely that your alarm clock will fail, but if your mobile phone battery runs out or you have a power cut in the night, you could be in trouble. It's better to be prepared for all eventualities, and the security in knowing you have a reserve wake-up call could aid a better night's sleep.

GET UP EARLY

For many people this may not be a problem, as the night before an exam may be a sleepless one. For those of you who have no trouble sleeping in, whatever the day has in store, remember that it is not every day that you have something as important as an exam to prepare yourself for. Having enough time to compose yourself and get ready calmly will help to keep you composed and maintain your focus.

TOP TIP

SPLISH SPLASH!

Feel revitalised and clean on the day so that you arrive for the exam feeling fresh and awake. A brisk shower will energise you for the day ahead, and the better you feel about yourself, the more confident you'll be in the exam.

GET THERE ON TIME

Make sure you prepare for all eventualities in getting to your exam – if you drive, leave early to allow for traffic; if you are relying on public transport, take an earlier bus or train than you think you need to allow for delays or missed connections. Many establishments have strict policies about arriving late for exams and most will not let you sit the exam if your lateness stretches beyond a certain period – sometimes this is simply once the exam has begun.

NO TALKING!

Avoid talking about the exam subject on the morning of the exam – it will only make you stressed. Somebody is bound to mention a topic you are not feeling confident about and it will not help your peace of mind.

OUTSIDE THE EXAMINATION ROOM

Right outside the exam room can be a horrendous place to spend the final minutes before you sit an exam. Inevitably there will be people brimming with confidence who may throw you off your stride by claiming to have revised everything possible and thus begin to plant seeds of doubt in your mind. Ignore these people by focusing inwardly on remaining calm and composed. Close your mind to external noises and distractions and breathe deeply.

DON'T REREAD YOUR NOTES

If you have successfully stuck to a well-planned revision schedule then you should not really be rereading any revision notes before you enter an exam. The time is better spent focusing your mind and trying to remain calm. You may also find that rereading your notes causes you to feel tense, especially if you read something you are unsure of. It is too late to learn anything new at this point.

THE EXAM ROOM

Exam candidates will experience a variety of emotions, from nervous anxiety to a dead-calm fatalism, to a quiet confidence – hopefully after following the advice in this book, the latter is what you'll achieve, but all of these emotions are normal. You can use your coping techniques to help you focus on the challenge ahead. Just try to find your seat, sit down, focus your mind and avoid talking to anyone else or looking around.

DURING THE EXAM

You've made it to the exam room – now it's time to put all you've learnt into practice.

LISTEN TO THE INSTRUCTIONS

It is really important to pay attention to the instructions given at the start of any exam. Invigilators may be divulging some important last-minute information. They may give details on entering candidate numbers or course codes etc. All of your hard work could be in vain if the examiners cannot correctly identify you by the details you provide.

WRITE LEGIBLY

Take your time and make sure that your handwriting and presentation is clear. Examiners cannot award marks for something they cannot read, no matter how good a point you make.

USE THE RIGHT PEN

Don't use red or green ink in your work. Some people may find it clearer, but spare a thought for the examiner. It will be quite infuriating for them if you present your work in the colour with which they wish to mark it! Exam boards usually stipulate which colours and even types of pen are acceptable, so be sure to find this out prior to the exam.

PUT PEN TO PAPER

The most difficult hurdle in any exam is writing the first few words, whatever the type of question. It is better to write something and correct it later than to spend ages thinking about the perfect introduction.

TOP TIP

READ THE QUESTION

Make sure you read the exact wording of the question – in fact, read it twice. If it is asking you 'who', don't respond with an answer to 'why'. Work out exactly what the question requires, and the respond.

ANSWER CAREFULLY

The questions may not be structured exactly as you would like, but you must make sure you answer what is asked of you and not what you would like to be asked. There is no point writing everything you know about a certain topic just to demonstrate the amount of information you have learnt. You will only gain marks for relevant information.

NO PEEKING!

Looking around to see what your friends are doing in an exam hall will only serve to distract them and you, and you will most likely be heavily penalised if the invigilator catches you. They may think you're trying to communicate with other students, so it's just not worth the risk.

JOGGING YOUR MEMORY

If you can't remember a fact or a name, try singing to yourself, doodling or even writing down the entire alphabet – it may be just the trigger you need.

CLEAR IT UP

When you are writing your answers and later checking what you have written, always check the clarity of your work. Examiners do not have time to interpret any ambiguities in your work or fathom your intentions. For instance, if you are referring to multiple sources in your work, make sure you identify each clearly, and if you've struggled trying to explain a complicated concept, now's the time to go back and try to reword it in order to simplify your answer.

PAY ATTENTION TO SPELLING

Check your spelling and grammar throughout, as you could be marked down and you risk the examiner misinterpreting your answer. Make sure your answers are as clear as possible.

TOP TIP

DON'T PANIC

If you find yourself getting agitated, fidgeting or hyperventilating, put down your pen, have a drink of water, close your eyes and relax for a few moments. It is more productive to rest for a while and resume work in a calm and assured manner than to try to get some coherent thoughts down on paper whilst feeling wound up.

HALF A MARK IS BETTER THAN NO MARK

Make sure you try to write something for every question or problem in the exam. It is better to attempt an answer and achieve a partial credit than to leave a blank space in the hope of making marks up on other questions. Remember, you'll always get zero if you don't attempt an answer, and every mark helps!

PLAN FOR POINTS

If you are running out of time and can see you won't be able to write down everything you'd like to, writing rough plans for answers to any remaining questions may gain you valuable marks — list your main points for anything you haven't covered, to show how your answer would have been completed.

TIME MANAGEMENT

When in the exam, divide up the available time appropriately, leaving more time to spend on questions with more marks allocated to them. It may seem obvious, but candidates frequently forget this important step. It may help to focus on the high-mark questions first, so that you can leap straight in and are sure not to run out of time (but don't get so carried away that you forget about the other questions!).

DON'T REPEAT

When answering the questions, there is no need to repeat the exact wording of the question you have been asked. The examiner knows what the question is and you won't receive any extra marks for it. Be careful, also, not to make the same point simply using slightly different wording – it just wastes time, so have the confidence that the examiner will have understood your point the first time around. You must be concise in your responses. If the question requires a one-word answer, then that is what you must give.

SHOW YOUR WORKINGS

If you are doing calculations, make it absolutely clear to the examiner how you arrived at the answer. The right answer is often only a small percentage of your mark and it is the working out that carries the most weighting. However, don't camouflage your page with scribbles, arrows and crossings out – you are usually allowed extra sheets for working out. Take advantage of these and make your work on the exam paper easily decipherable.

CHECK AND RECHECK

Once you have finished an exam, do reread and recheck your work. Examiners appreciate fluency and coherence in answer structure and this can only be gauged by reading what you have written in its entirety. A missed word or a garbled sentence could scupper your otherwise well-crafted answer. Plan to allow time at the end of the exam session to check your answers.

HAND IN ON TIME

There are nearly always penalties for failing to put your pen down when instructed, so make sure that, whatever stage you are at with your answer, you really do put your pen down as soon as the allocated time is up. It's unlikely you'll gain any points from a few extra words, and it's not worth risking being penalised for not adhering to the rules.

AFTER THE EXAM

Congratulations! It's all over... now what?

IT'S ALL OVER

Don't waste time mulling over what could have been. If you have revised thoroughly, the chances are that your results will reflect this. It is either time to go out and celebrate or, if you have more exams, forget about the one you've just done (phew, a load off your mind!) and concentrate on excelling in the next one.

DON'T DISCUSS IT

Getting involved in discussing what your peers have written or how they answered questions can only sow seeds of doubt in your mind, and theirs. It can make you feel vulnerable and inadequate. No two people will have answered questions in exactly the same way, so the safest thing to do is to avoid talking about it and discuss your post-exam celebrations instead.

WHY PEOPLE FAIL

There are lots of reasons why people might fail an exam, but here are a few of the most common causes, and things you can do to prevent them happening to you.

TOP TIP

IDENTIFY YOUR WEAK POINTS

It can be useful to familiarise yourself with the main causes of failure, so you can identify whether you are likely to suffer from any weak spots you may have. If so, you should spend extra time working on these things in the lead-up to your test to make sure you're confident enough to avoid any of these pitfalls.

RELYING ON LUCK

Some people take exams hoping for a fluke, but taking exams isn't about luck; it's about hard work and focused effort. Simply attending lectures probably won't be enough. By working through this book and revising efficiently, you will be able to walk into the exam room prepared.

YOUR REVISION ONLY FOCUSED ON ONE TOPIC

You are unlikely to achieve your best result in an exam if you simply revise one or two of the topics in the syllabus and hope that they are included in the exam. Success depends on thorough revision and studying a broad spectrum of topics. Revising a greater cross-section of topics will help you avoid this.

THE PRESSURE IS BUILDING

Don't spend time reflecting upon the implications that passing or failing a course will have on the rest of your life. If the exam is crucial to qualify in a chosen career, or in moving on to the next level of education in a chosen institution, the added pressure can often distract from the need to knuckle down and study. Put things into perspective – if you've worked hard there's no reason why you should fail. Remind yourself that in the unlikely event that you do fail, you can usually apply to re-sit the exam.

TOO MUCH CONFIDENCE

Overconfidence breeds complacency. This is a dangerous mentality to adopt and can lead to disappointment on results day. You can never be too prepared for an exam and people who give a great impression of overconfidence are often disguising a lack of good preparation.

NOT STICKING TO THE TIMETABLE

It is impossible to stress enough that a successful revision programme depends on sticking to a revision timetable. Try not to obsess over one subject, or to ignore it completely, but stick to the balanced timetable you have worked out. A balance of subject matter, combined with a sensible structure of relaxation and study, is vital.

THE GLASS IS HALF EMPTY

When you're feeling full of despair, it's often tempting to do nothing, believing that nothing you do today can make any overall difference. But it really is worth putting in a bit of effort each day – even if it's only ten minutes. Those little sessions will add up, and you'll be surprised what a good effect a little bit of studying can have on your mood. You'll get the ball rolling, and soon you'll find yourself able to tackle half-hour sessions of revision like the best of them.

GOOD LUCK!

Like it or not, exam-taking is a fundamental part of education and being well prepared for taking exams is of massive importance. Start early, spread out your workload and try to stay relaxed during the whole process. A bit of careful planning goes a long way, and if you are methodical and organised you will find the whole process easier to tackle. Good revision and exam technique will reduce your stress levels, increase your feelings of confidence in the exam room, and set you well on the way to success.

Good luck!

If you're interested in finding out more about our books, find us on Facebook at **Summersdale Publishers** and follow us on Twitter at **@Summersdale**.

www.summersdale.com